COLUMBUS DIDN'T DISCOVER AMERICA

EXPOSING MYTHS ABOUT EXPLORERS IN THE AMERICAS

BY JANEY LEVY

Gareth Stevens
PUBLISHING

Please visit our website, www.garethstevens.com. For a free color catalog of all our high quality books, call toll free 1-800-542-2595 or fax 1-877-542-2596.

Cataloging-in-Publication Data

Names: Levy, Janey.
Title: Columbus didn't discover America: exposing myths about explorers in the Americas / Janey Levy.
Description: New York : Gareth Stevens Publishing, 2020. | Series: Exposed! more myths about American history | Includes glossary and index.
Identifiers: ISBN 9781538237427 (pbk.) | ISBN 9781538237441 (library bound) | ISBN 9781538237434 (6 pack)
Subjects: LCSH: Columbus, Christopher–Juvenile literature. | America–Discovery and exploration–Spanish–Juvenile literature.
Classification: LCC E111.L48 2020 | DDC 970.01'5092–dc23
First Edition

Published in 2020 by
Gareth Stevens Publishing
111 East 14th Street, Suite 349
New York, NY 10003

Copyright © 2020 Gareth Stevens Publishing

Designer: Sarah Liddell
Editor: Therese Shea

Photo credits: Cover, p. 1 John Vanderlyn/Davepape/Wikimedia Commons; background texture used throughout IS MODE/Shutterstock.com; ripped newspaper used throughout STILLFX/Shutterstock.com; photo corners used throughout Carolyn Franks/Shutterstock.com; p. 5 Print Collector/Contributor/Hulton Archive/Getty Images; p. 7 Alonso de Mendoza/Wikimedia Commons; p. 9 Peter Hermes Furian/Shutterstock.com; p. 11 (map) Heritage Images/Contributor/Hulton Archive/Getty Images; p. 11 (Earth) NASA/GSFC/Reto Stockli, Nazmi El Saleous, and Matt Jentoft-Nilsen/Shizhao/Wikimedia Commons; p. 13 Joe Sohm/Visions of America/Universal Images Group/Getty Images; p. 15 (house) D. Gordon E. Robertson/Dger/Wikimedia Commons; p. 15 (statue) Steven Pavlov/Senapa/Wikimedia Commons; p. 17 Bettmann/Contributor/Bettmann/Getty Images; p. 19 (main) Heritage Images/Contributor/Hulton Archive/Getty Images; p. 19 (Quetzacóatl) Eddo/Wikimedia Commons; p. 21 (main) Photo 12/Contributor/Universal Images Group/Getty Images; p. 21 (inset) John Martin PERRY/Unbuttered Parsnip/Wikimedia Commons; pp. 23 (de Soto), 25 (Daniel Boone) Stock Montage/Contributor/Archive Photos/Getty Images; p. 23 (Ozark Mountains) Roschetzky Photography/Shutterstock.com; p. 25 (Boone burial site) Nagel Photography/Shutterstock.com; p. 27 (Lewis and Clark) Charles Willson Peale/Crisco 1492/Wikimedia Commons; p. 27 (Sacagawea) Ace Diamond/Shutterstock.com.

Printed in the United States of America

CPSIA compliance information: Batch #CS19GS: For further information contact Gareth Stevens, New York, New York at 1-800-542-2595.

CONTENTS

Words in the glossary appear in **bold** type the first time they are used in the text.

WHAT REALLY HAPPENED?

You may have heard stories about famous **explorers** in the Americas. Christopher Columbus discovered America. Juan Ponce de León searched for the Fountain of Youth. The Aztecs of Mexico thought Hernán Cortés was one of their gods returning to them.

These stories are often presented as fact. But are they actually true? Or are they **myths** that have been repeated so often people accept them as fact? It's time to dig deeper into some of the "facts" about these well-known explorers.

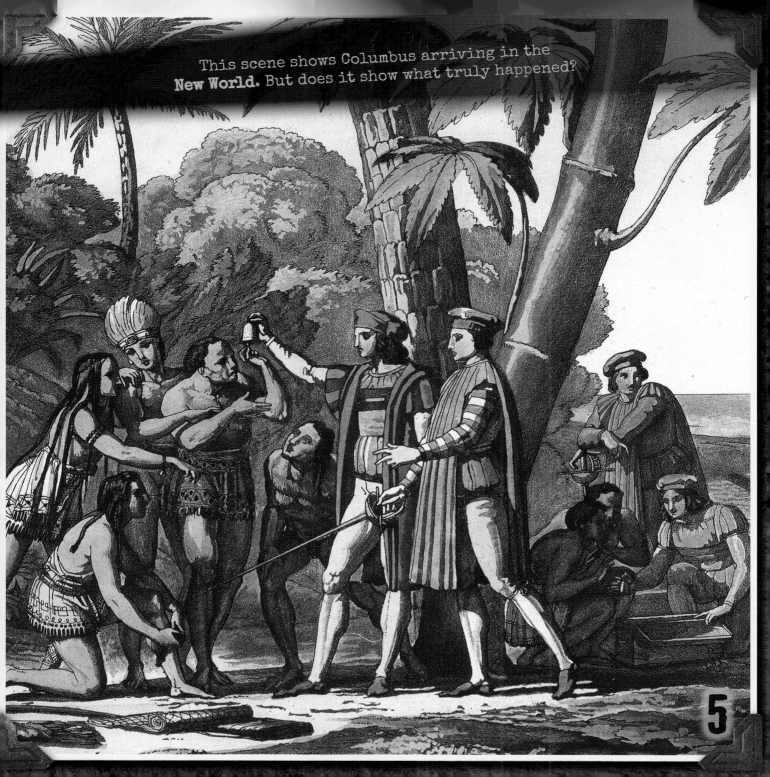

This scene shows Columbus arriving in the **New World.** But does it show what truly happened?

5

THE COLUMBUS MYTHS

THE MYTH: CHRISTOPHER COLUMBUS DISCOVERED AMERICA IN 1492.

THE FACTS:

To "discover" something is to find it for the first time. Christopher Columbus didn't discover the land we know today as America. It had already been found thousands of years earlier by the **ancestors** of today's Native Americans. By the time Columbus landed in the New World, millions of people lived there.

Columbus wasn't even the first European explorer to reach the New World. **Vikings** had reached North America hundreds of years earlier.

WHO SAW THE SAINT LAWRENCE FIRST?

It's often claimed that French explorer Jacques Cartier discovered Canada's Saint Lawrence River in 1534. But, like Columbus, he couldn't discover something native peoples had known about for centuries.

This picture of Columbus, completed in 1519, was painted about 13 years after his death.

COLUMBUS LANDED IN NORTH AMERICA.

THE FACTS:

Columbus made four voyages, or trips, to the New World, but he never reached the North American **continent**.

On his first voyage, he landed in the group of islands now known as the Bahamas. He later landed on several islands in or near the Caribbean Sea, including those now known as Cuba, Hispaniola (Haiti and the Dominican Republic), and Jamaica. He also landed on the coast of what is now Venezuela in South America.

ISN'T THIS THE EAST INDIES?

Columbus never recognized he'd landed in the New World. He had been trying to reach the East Indies—part of Asia—and always believed that's what he'd done.

THE
BAHAMAS

ATLANTIC OCEAN

CUBA

DOMINICAN
REPUBLIC

HAITI

JAMAICA

CARIBBEAN SEA

VENEZUELA

Columbus came close to the North American continent and the country
now called the United States, but he never landed there.

9

THE MYTH: COLUMBUS WANTED TO PROVE EARTH ISN'T FLAT.

THE FACTS:

Many in Columbus's day knew that Earth is round. As early as the 6th century BC, ancient Greek thinkers had written that Earth was a sphere, or ball, shape. Columbus even owned a copy of an ancient book that talked about the shape of Earth.

Books published in Europe between 1200 and 1500 also said that Earth is round. By Columbus's time, most educated people knew about Earth's shape.

PRETTY BIG PLANET

The problem for Columbus wasn't the shape of Earth. It was that he thought Earth was much smaller than it is and that Asia was just on the other side of the Atlantic Ocean from Europe.

11

THE MYTH:

COLUMBUS'S SHIPS WERE NAMED THE *NIÑA*, THE *PINTA*, AND THE *SANTA MARÍA*.

THE FACTS:

Sailors commonly called their ships by **nicknames** they had given them. The real name of the *Niña* was likely *Santa Clara*. The nickname is thought to come from the name of the ship's owner, Juan Niño.

No one knows what the *Pinta*'s real name was. *Santa María* was that ship's real name, but the sailors called it *La Gallega*, after the territory of Galicia in Spain where the ship was built.

CABOT, CATHAY, AND CANADA

John Cabot, exploring for England, did manage to reach North America, landing in Canada in 1497—but, like Columbus, he believed he'd reached Asia. To be exact, Cabot thought he'd reached China, which was known as Cathay then.

These full-size copies of Columbus's ships let people today see what it was like to be on one of these ships.

THE MYTH: VIKING EXPLORER LEIF ERIKSON WAS THE FIRST EUROPEAN TO SEE NORTH AMERICA.

THE FACTS:

Leif Erikson landed in North America around the year 1000. Ruins of a Viking settlement from that time have been found in what is now Newfoundland, Canada. The settlement has been named L'Anse aux Meadows. This is the oldest known European settlement in the New World.

However, it's NOT the first time a European saw North America! A Viking named Bjarni Herjólfsson saw the coast of North America in 986.

ACCIDENTAL EXPLORER

It was completely by accident that Bjarni Herjólfsson saw the coast of North America. He was sailing from Iceland to Greenland when storms blew him off course.

STATUE OF LEIF ERIKSON

This is a reconstruction of a Viking house at L'Anse aux Meadows in Newfoundland, Canada.

THE FABLED FOUNTAIN OF YOUTH

THE MYTH: JUAN PONCE DE LEÓN SEARCHED FOR THE FOUNTAIN OF YOUTH.

THE FACTS:

Juan Ponce de León was a Spanish **conquistador** (kahn-KEE-stah-dor). There's nothing in any of Ponce de León's writings about the Fountain of Youth. There's nothing about it in the writings of others connected with his **expedition** either.

Ponce de León's contracts from the Spanish king say nothing about such an object. What Ponce de León and the king both wanted was wealth and power—gold, land, and control over the native peoples in the area.

According to the story, the Fountain of Youth would give endless life to anyone who bathed in it or drank from it.

THE LAST LAUGH

The story that Ponce de León was searching for the Fountain of Youth was started by his enemies after his death. They wanted to make the conquistador look foolish.

17

THE MYTH:

THE AZTECS OF MEXICO BELIEVED HERNÁN CORTÉS WAS A GOD RETURNING TO THEM.

THE FACTS:

Quetzalcóatl (keht-sahl-koh-WAH-tehl), shown as a feathered snake, was one of the main Aztec gods. Some said the Aztecs believed Cortés was Quetzalcóatl when he arrived in 1519. However, there's no evidence, or proof, of this.

Cortés never said anything about Quetzalcóatl in any of his writings. He never said anything about being mistaken for any god. There's also no evidence the Aztecs believed Quetzalcóatl would return to them from the East.

MADE-UP HISTORY

The story that the Aztecs believed Cortés was Quetzalcóatl first appeared many years after Cortés arrived. It was made up by people to serve their own purposes.

QUETZALCÓATL

This shows an artist's idea of what the first meeting between Cortés and the Aztec leader Montezuma II may have been like.

A JOB FOR MEN?

THE MYTH:
ALL CONQUISTADORS WERE MEN.

THE FACTS:

It's true that most conquistadors were men. But some Spanish women accompanied the conquistadors. And some of those women fought alongside them!

The most famous was María de Estrada, also known as the Great Lady. She and her husband joined Cortés's expedition to Mexico. She fought in every battle and is believed to have been skilled with the sword. Other female conquistadors were Beatriz Bermúdez de Velasco and Inés de Suárez.

María de Estrada fought with Cortés when he took over the Aztec capital and **conquered** the Aztecs. For her service, Cortés gave her control of two towns.

This is how a conquistador would have dressed for battle.

A TALE OF TREASURE

THE MYTH: SPANISH CONQUISTADOR HERNANDO DE SOTO HID GOLDEN TREASURE IN THE OZARK MOUNTAINS OF ARKANSAS.

THE FACTS:

Hernando de Soto *did* enter what is today Arkansas in 1541. He and his soldiers were the first Europeans to come to the area.

But he never reached the bluff, or cliff, **shelters** in the Ozarks where some people say he hid gold. We know this because three of de Soto's men left behind written accounts that tell exactly where they went as they traveled through Arkansas.

WHERE'S THE GOLD?

Far from hiding gold in the Ozarks, de Soto was looking for gold and other riches. But there were no gold and riches to be found, and de Soto died of fever in 1542 by the banks of the Mississippi River.

HERNANDO DE SOTO

OZARK MOUNTAINS

De Soto began the expedition that brought him to Arkansas with about 600 men. About half the men were killed in battle with Native Americans or died of illnesses.

23

THE FICTIONAL FRONTIERSMAN

THE MYTH: DANIEL BOONE WORE A CAP MADE FROM RACCOON SKIN AND FUR.

THE FACTS:

Boone is remembered as a hunter and explorer. But he didn't like raccoon-skin caps and never wore one. He preferred hats made from beaver skin and fur.

Boone was also more than the 18th-century **frontiersman** people imagine. He was a military leader, store owner, farmer, and Virginia lawmaker. And unlike many frontiersmen, he could read and write. He loved to read, and one of his favorite books was *Gulliver's Travels*.

FAMOUS FIGHTER?

Although stories tell of Daniel Boone as an Indian fighter, he said he fought Native Americans only when he had to. He claimed he had killed three Indians in his life, and he was sorry because Native Americans had treated him better than white people.

DANIEL BOONE

It's possible that the body buried in Daniel Boone's grave, shown here, wasn't Boone's. The body was thought to have been moved from one grave to another—but the wrong body may have been dug up!

HEROES OR FAILURES?

THE MYTH: THE LEWIS AND CLARK EXPEDITION TO EXPLORE THE LOUISIANA TERRITORY WAS A GREAT SUCCESS.

THE FACTS:

In 1804, an expedition led by Meriwether Lewis and William Clark set out to explore the Louisiana Territory. Its main goal was to find a water route, or path, to the Pacific Ocean. It didn't accomplish that. In fact, it didn't establish any routes to the West.

The route Lewis and Clark took was too hard for settlers to follow. Lewis also failed to write his planned account of their journey. People forgot about the expedition for years.

Lewis and Clark's expedition wasn't a total failure. Lewis recorded 178 plants and 122 animals that hadn't been known in the East. They also created new maps.

WILLIAM CLARK

MERIWETHER LEWIS

SACAGAWEA

THANKS, SACAGAWEA!

In 1902, a writer looking for a strong female hero to use in her book learned of Lewis and Clark's Native American guide, Sacagawea. Her book became a best seller, and Sacagawea's popularity helped people learn about Lewis and Clark.

27

KEEP INQUIRING

As you read stories about explorers, ask questions. How do we know these "facts" are true? What's the evidence? Are there written accounts to support them? Can we trust the written accounts? Were the writers actually there? Did they understand the unfamiliar people they met? Did they have reasons to lie? Is there **physical** evidence, such as the ruins at L'Anse aux Meadows?

Learning history takes effort, but it's worth it. It helps us understand how we became who we are today!

A TIMELINE OF EXPLORERS IN THE AMERICAS

986: BJARNI HERJÓLFSSON SEES THE COAST OF NORTH AMERICA.

C. 1000: LEIF ERIKSON LANDS IN NORTH AMERICA.

1492: CHRISTOPHER COLUMBUS REACHES THE AMERICAS.

1497: JOHN CABOT LANDS IN CANADA.

1499: AMERIGO VESPUCCI MAKES HIS FIRST VOYAGE TO SOUTH AMERICA.

1513: JUAN PONCE DE LEÓN LANDS IN FLORIDA.

1513: VASCO NÚÑEZ DE BALBOA CROSSES PANAMA AND SEES THE PACIFIC OCEAN.

1521: HERNÁN CORTÉS CONQUERS THE AZTECS.

1534: JACQUES CARTIER EXPLORES THE SAINT LAWRENCE RIVER.

1539: HERNANDO DE SOTO BEGINS EXPLORING THE AMERICAN SOUTHEAST.

1540: FRANCISCO VÁSQUEZ DE CORONADO EXPLORES MEXICO AND THE AMERICAN SOUTHWEST.

1603: SAMUEL DE CHAMPLAIN BEGINS EXPLORING NORTH AMERICA.

1769: DANIEL BOONE BEGINS EXPLORING KENTUCKY.

1804: MERIWETHER LEWIS AND WILLIAM CLARK SET OUT TO EXPLORE THE LOUISIANA TERRITORY.

These are just some of the major explorers of the Americas. Many people explored them, and explorations continued until well into the 19th century.

GLOSSARY

ancestor: someone in your family who lived long before you

conquer: to take by force

conquistador: a Spanish conqueror or adventurer

continent: one of Earth's seven great landmasses

expedition: a trip made for a certain purpose

explorer: one who searches in order to find out new things

frontiersman: a person who lives on the edge of settled territory

myth: an idea or story that is believed by many people but that is not true

New World: the name given by Europeans to North, Central, and South America

nickname: a name that is different from your real name but is what some people call you

physical: existing in a form that you can touch or see

shelter: a place where animals or people are kept safe

Viking: a person from far northern Europe who attacked the coasts of Europe in the 8th to 10th centuries

FOR MORE INFORMATION

BOOKS

Macdonald, Fiona. *You Wouldn't Want to Sail with Christopher Columbus! Uncharted Waters You'd Rather Not Cross.* New York, NY: Franklin Watts, 2014.

Sansevere-Dreher, Diane. *Explorers Who Got Lost.* New York, NY: Starscape, 2016.

WEBSITES

Exploration
www.history.com/topics/exploration
Find links to information about many explorers as well as possible "discoverers" of America.

Famous Explorers
www.mrnussbaum.com/explorers/famous-explorers/
Learn more about famous explorers from different countries.

World Explorers
www.ducksters.com/biography/explorers/
Read about the reasons people explore.

INDEX